Genre-Based Writing

Genre-Based Writing

What Every ESL Teacher Needs to Know

By

Christine M. Tardy
University of Arizona

University of Michigan Press
Ann Arbor

First paperback edition 2023
Copyright © Christine M. Tardy, 2019
All rights reserved
Published in the United States of America by the
University of Michigan Press

Paperback ISBN: 978-0-472-03958-6
Ebook ISBN: 978-0-472-12626-2

First published March 2019

ACKNOWLEDGMENTS

I am most grateful to Kelly Sippell, editor extraordinaire, for seeing a place for this ebook, for her guidance throughout its preparation, and for her ongoing commitment to building the pool of teacher resources in our profession. I would also like to thank my colleagues Erin Whittig and Alan Kohler for their time reading an earlier version of this manuscript and for providing invaluable feedback. They are inspiring teachers and teacher educators whose feedback been critical in the revision process. Remaining weaknesses are mine alone. I also thank Matthew and Benjamin for their constant love and support, even when I'm taking on too many projects. Finally, I need to acknowledge that the ideas offered in this book could not possibly be the property of one person. I have learned so much from my many teaching colleagues, mentors, mentees, and students over the years. Their insights and inspirational classroom work inform every aspect of this book, and I am indebted to their collaborations and inspiring practices.

CONTENTS

Introduction

In the mid-1990s, after completing my MA-TESL degree, I went to Japan to teach English. I had found a good job teaching at a Japanese English for Specific Purposes (ESP) company. It turned out that all of my teaching during my three years in Japan was at a large multinational U.S.-owned company, whose Far East headquarters were located in Kobe. My courses focused mainly on oral communication and common activities that the students (mostly scientific researchers) needed to carry out in English: participating in meetings, presenting research, entertaining guests, and so on. After a year or so, though, I was asked to help teach the memo writing class that had been developed by two of my colleagues. Having taught academic writing as an MA student, I was excited to teach writing in this new context.

I quickly learned more than I ever thought I would about the various paper and shampoo products of the company, as I read through the students' on-the-job research memos. At first, the writing seemed odd and a little clumsy to me. It wasn't ungrammatical, but it adopted strange phrases, provided limited background information, and sometimes consisted almost entirely of graphs or tables and bulleted lists. It certainly wasn't like any writing I was familiar with, but these unusual features were not just examples of the students' misconceptions of how to write; they were also found in the "model" memos that were collected from the students' managers.

Although I had learned about genre and genre-based pedagogy as an undergraduate and an MA student, this experience in Japan was the light-bulb moment that made me realize the value of genre in teaching writing. When I later developed a second memo-writing class for the students at this multinational company, I became immersed in their in-company writing. What I had once seen as strange idiosyncrasies, I came to understand as local preferences and expectations. In order to write effectively for their managers, my students did not need to learn thesis statements, topic sentences, or citation practices—they needed to learn in-company norms for announcing purpose, organizing and presenting research findings, and clearly stating recommended actions. Genre became a key concept for my own acceptance that these very different norms were indeed what my students needed (in fact, wanted) to learn, and genre-based pedagogy provided an essential approach to designing and teaching my course.

Since that time in the 1990s, I have mostly taught academic writing rather than professional writing, but the lessons I learned in Japan have been equally applicable to the other teaching contexts I have found myself in. Whether working with international graduate students in the U.S., business undergraduates in Turkey, or first-year students at U.S. universities, genre has proven productive for me and my students, helping us to learn about writing preferences within specific rhetorical situations—and to consider how to adapt or even bend those conventions when needed.

Despite my own positive experiences with genre-based pedagogies in second language writing classrooms, teachers often tell me at conferences that they wish they understood genre better, or that they find the term a little confusing. My hope is that this book might offer an accessible introduction to genre and genre-based writing instruction. It is, in many ways, the culmination of years of my own pedagogical experimentations in the classroom, numerous workshops with new and experienced teachers, and various theoretical and empirical explorations of genre and genre-based teaching.

Implementing genre-based teaching involves an understanding of genre, an understanding of key principles of genre-based pedagogy, and tools for putting those principles into practice. This book addresses all three of these concerns, beginning with an overview of genre and genre-based teaching (the first three chapters). Chapters 4–6 provide suggestions and illustrations for developing genre-based tasks in a writing classroom, focusing on various dimensions of genre: form, content, social practices, and rhetorical situation. The final two chapters consider how playful exploitations of genre may be implemented in the classroom and share final tips for L2 writing teachers. Sample classroom activities are found throughout the text; while many of these tasks derive from my own experiences teaching adults in academic contexts, I hope that they provide inspiration for teachers from a range of settings as they create their own genre-based tasks.

1. What Is Genre?

Genre in Popular Culture

The term **genre** is familiar to most people. We commonly use it to describe categories of books, music, film, and art. As a result, most teachers and students already have a general sense of genre as a category. This understanding is a good starting point, even if it is not necessarily an ideal end point.

In film, for instance, we may think of drama, horror, action, comedy, thriller, romance, or westerns as a general way to classify movies. Within those broad categories, we find more specific sub-genres; horror movies may include slashers, zombies, paranormal, or psychological thrillers. We can also find hybrid genres, such as romantic comedies or mockumentaries.

These various categories are meaningful to moviegoers because they give a sense of what to expect when they go to a movie in a specific category. When prompted, my students are usually able to identify common characteristics of a genre like a slasher movie pretty easily. The story typically revolves around a killer seeking revenge for past trauma. It takes place mostly in dark settings and often involves a group of young people who each take turns going to places that most people would avoid and then fatally encountering the frightening killer. In most slashers, only one or two main characters survive, often a young woman. Slashers generally also feature scary music and surprises that make the audience jump. These common features are also called **conventions**—they have become so common within the genre that audiences expect them, and their presence also gives the audience clues about what kind of genre they are watching.

Of course, slasher movies are usually not very relevant to teaching writing, but the notion of genre certainly is.

Genre in Academic Writing

The basic idea of genre as a category is useful for academic writing, just like it is for forms of art, film, or music. Genre helps us to sort different types of writing, to understand how they differ, and to identify common features or conventions of a particular genre. For students, genre offers a lens or frame for understanding what makes writing effective in different situations and contexts.

Consider the question "What is good writing?" When I pose this question to students, they often respond by describing good writing with words like *clear*, *well organized*, or *interesting*. These are pretty general terms, so I like to press them further. Sometimes I show them an excerpt from an article published in a top science journal, such as the *BMJ*. Typically, they do not find the writing clear at all, and they cannot understand the content well enough to know if it is well organized or interesting. We discuss whether they *think* it might be good writing—and *for whom*? This prompts an interesting discussion about the purpose of the writing, as well as the readers and authors in a particular case, and how those participants might evaluate the quality of the text. Sometimes I show my students interesting or humorous protest signs and ask if they think that is good writing. Protest signs involve limited organization, and the texts themselves are often not "clear" in any traditional sense (relying heavily on references to events not explained in the sign). But students often can agree that some signs are "good writing" in some way.

These conversations help us move toward the notion of genre while avoiding overly technical terminology. When we think about writing as occurring primarily through different genres—from to-do lists to thank-you notes to lab reports to research articles—we start to see that writing is quite varied, and that our evaluations of writing (much like our evaluations for movies) depend largely on the extent to which a text fulfills our expectations for its genre.

Genre has been defined in different ways by scholars in applied linguistics and rhetoric and composition studies, though they share a similar focus on genre as a category of social practice and form. Martin's (1984) definition of genre is "a staged, goal-oriented, purposeful activity in which speakers engage as members of our culture" (p. 25). Swales (1990) has defined genre as "a class of communicative events" (p. 45), in which language plays a significant role. He notes that genres have "a shared set of communicative purposes" (p. 46) and that examples of a genre share some kind of "family resemblance" (p. 49). In many cases, we can point to prototypical examples of a genre, though genres always leave room for variation—some genres are more liberal in this way than others.

As both of these definitions emphasize, genres are used and shaped by communities (sometimes referred to as **discourse communities**). Genres are used by social groups, or discourse communities, to carry out repeated activities: wedding invitations, instruction manuals, eulogies, lecture slides, public apologies, lab reports, or social media birthday wishes are all examples of genres. The communities that use a genre may be quite large or more tightly knit.

It is also useful to emphasize that genres *do* things, typically responding to common situations (also referred to as **rhetorical situations**). For instance, when people apply for jobs, in many contexts, they need others to vouch for them, confirming that they are suitable applicants. As this situation recurred over time, people developed similar ways of responding—thus, the emergence of the letter of recommendation. Genres become more "typified" or regularized as more and more users recognize common ways of responding to similar situations. These common forms are referred to as **conventions**.

One important principle that different genre definitions share is that genres are not defined by their form but instead by their purposes—that is, by the actions that they aim to carry out (Miller, 1984). A thank-you note, for example, responds to a particular social situation: receiving a gift or a special act of kindness. We would not write a thank-you note for just *any* gift. I am unlikely to write one if someone gives me a candy bar, but I probably would write one if someone bought me an expensive gift or substitute-taught my class for me. And, importantly, the practices surrounding the genre of thank-you notes often vary by community. In my own family, thank-you notes are common and expected, while my husband's family generally sees thank-you notes as unnecessary amongst family members.

This example of a thank-you note also shows that learning to use a genre involves much more than learning its form. The form is just one part of the social practice (or social action) that the genre carries out. When we use a genre like a thank-you note, we adopt specific social practices and values. Over time and with experience, we learn to carry out those practices—including the related genres—in ways that are considered appropriate within communities of users. These practices might include:

- when or if to use the genre (e.g., *Is a thank-you note needed in this particular instance? Would it be better to make a phone call?*)
- the appropriate timing of sharing the genre (e.g., *How soon should the note be sent?*)
- the appropriate mode of doing so (e.g., *Can a thank-you note be sent as an email? Should it be sent through the mail or can it be hand-delivered?*).

We learn to use a range of genres in everyday life: thank-you notes, grocery lists, to-do lists, emails of apology, "I'm running late" texts, and more formal genres like wedding invitations, consumer complaints, or eulogies.

We typically learn to use these genres through exposure, practice, and informal (or even implicit) feedback from others. Over time, we develop a sense of how to use genres appropriately in different circumstances and with different people. Sometimes this "sense" can be learned simply through observing and participating, but in other cases, explicit feedback or guidance is needed.

Just like everyday genres, academic genres are also forms of social practice. One challenge with academic genres, however, is that we don't use them as commonly as we use everyday genres, nor do we tend to see as many examples. In addition, academic genres are often very complex and may rely not just on knowledge of social practice (of teachers, researchers, scholars, and professors), but also on highly specific subject-matter knowledge. Many academic genres are written in evaluative settings in which outcomes such as grades, funding, or even degrees are dependent on the genre's success.

Examples of Genres

Just as with film genres, we can think of written genres (including academic genres) along different levels, and scholars do not always agree on these levels or classification systems. One way to classify academic genres is through broad categories, sometimes called **elemental genres**, such as:

- procedure
- narrative
- description
- report
- explanation

These categories describe "rhetorical structures fundamental to various forms of communication in a culture" (Hyland, 2004, p. 29). Teachers often think in terms of these broad-level genre categories when creating writing assignments. These categories are common in writing textbooks and are all relatively prominent types of texts in school-based writing.

But genres can also be categorized more narrowly, and getting to this level of specificity can be helpful for highlighting the goals, audiences, and conventions of a genre in closer detail. For example, within the broad category of narratives, we find genres like:

- literacy narratives
- autobiographies
- memoirs

- travel stories
- histories of an organization
- digital stories

Similarly, there are many genres that might fall under the category of argument:

- school-based argument essays
- op-ed pieces
- political blog posts
- infographics

When we look at genres at this more precise level, we see that they do not always fit neatly into just one broad-level category. Infographics, for example, could be considered a kind of argument genre, but they may also include characteristics of reports or explanations.

Academic contexts are filled with many different genres. In a history course, students might write analyses of historical documents or mock op-ed pieces "written" during an important moment in history. In a journalism course, students might write profiles or news reports. In an anthropology course, students might write a mini-ethnography. In a biology class, genres like lab reports or scientific posters are fairly common.

As students become more specialized in academic fields of study, the genres they write tend to change. Early schooling may include a fair amount of essay writing, but more advanced levels of education (especially graduate education) typically engage students in genres like case studies, research proposals, research or technical reports, or even dissertations.

APPLICATION ACTIVITY

It can be easy to confuse genre with form or even mode of communication. Focusing on the intended action or purpose of a text is therefore essential. An email, *for example, is not a genre but a form of communication; an* apology email *is a genre. In the following list, which items do you think could be considered a genre?*

- *blog*
- *author bio in book*
- *FAQs*
- *obituary*

- *social media*
- *text messages*
- *website*
- *weather report*

Compare your answers with someone else. For each item that you think is not a genre, can you identify more specific examples of that item that would be genres? For example, a website is a bit too broad to be considered a genre, but there are types of websites that are genres—what are some examples?

Why Is Genre Important for Writing Instruction?

There is no one recipe for "good writing." Throughout their education, students need to write in many different genres, each with their own sets of conventions and expectations. Doing so can be challenging, but the concept of genre offers a useful tool for supporting students in this endeavor.

When we view writing as occurring largely through genres, we shift away from over-generalized and static rules about writing. Genre turns our attention to the purpose(s) of the text, the readers and writers, the context(s) of use, and the related expectations for the text's form and content.

APPLICATION ACTIVITY

Make a list of the everyday genres that you wrote in last week. These might include things like to-do lists, specific types of emails, social media posts, etc. Next, make a list of all of the professional or academic genres that you wrote in last week. Looking through both lists, consider how you learned to write in these different genres. Are there any differences in how you learned everyday genres compared with professional or academic genres?

2. What Is a Genre-Based Approach to Teaching Writing?

What do we teach when we teach genre? Genre scholars typically focus on two related areas for teaching: genre knowledge and genre awareness. The good news for teachers is that many strategies of genre-based pedagogy can help students build *both* genre knowledge and genre awareness. This chapter describes each separately and then considers how they relate to each other. Finally, key principles of genre-based teaching are outlined.

Genre-Specific Knowledge

Genre knowledge is, in short, what a writer (or reader) knows about specific genres and the concept of genre more generally. Because genres are social practices and social actions, *knowing* a specific genre includes knowing more about it than simply what it looks like. The various dimensions of **genre-specific knowledge** (Tardy, 2009) include an understanding of:

- form (**formal knowledge**)
- how to act effectively with the rhetorical context (**rhetorical knowledge**)
- practices and processes for carrying out the genre (**process knowledge**)
- content (**subject-matter** or **content knowledge**)

Formal knowledge encompasses common conventions for language use, organizing information, mechanics, or even design. **Rhetorical knowledge** includes understanding the dynamics of the rhetorical context, such as what the genre is trying to accomplish and how, the values and practices of the genre's users, and even the social relations between the writer(s) and readers. **Process knowledge** is knowledge of how the genre is written, revised, delivered, read, and used. **Subject-matter knowledge** includes the writer's understanding of the content of the genre; in everyday genres, this content knowledge may be relatively mundane (e.g., your knowledge of what is in the refrigerator while composing a grocery list), but in academic or professional genres, content knowledge can require strong expertise in the subject matter.

Let's think through an example. A few months ago, I was asked to write an endorsement blurb for a forthcoming book on genre. The blurb would be quoted—in part or full—on the book's back cover and perhaps used in marketing materials. To write this blurb successfully, I had to marshal my various dimensions of genre knowledge.

Of course, I had to know what an endorsement blurb looks like (formal knowledge): how long it is, how formal or informal it is, and how much jargon might be useful, for example. I looked at several examples to get a sense of whether writers typically use first person, second person, or third person (or a mix) in these blurbs.

In considering my language choices, I also had to understand the rhetorical context (rhetorical knowledge). I thought about the goals of this genre (to encourage people to read the book, to praise the book), my relation to the authors (two genre scholars I greatly admire), and the disciplinary approaches to evaluation and praise (what is praiseworthy).

Related, I considered how and where people read endorsement blurbs (process knowledge). I knew that I read them when browsing book exhibits at conferences or when skimming the many book flyers I receive in my workplace mailbox. I knew I do not read blurbs carefully but rather look at them quickly, often noticing only who wrote them and what they said was especially good about the book.

Finally, to write my blurb, I drew upon my knowledge of the field of genre studies, the focus of the book I was endorsing (subject-matter knowledge). Based on my familiarity with this scholarship (and of the book itself), I considered what this new book added to the literature, how it was unique, and how it might be useful for different kinds of genre scholars.

This particular instance was only the second time I had written an endorsement blurb, but I was already somewhat familiar with the genre as a reader. Although I would not consider myself an expert in this genre by any means, it was not hard to write because I had prior knowledge to draw on. Someone from outside my field—say, from chemistry—might have much more difficulty. A chemist could probably figure out the preferred form of the blurb fairly easily, but understanding the rhetorical context might be harder since academic books are rare in chemistry. More importantly, the chemist would lack subject-matter knowledge of the field and the book's contents, making it very difficult to know what to write about in the blurb.

This extended example shows that there is a lot to learn about genres, which is why they can be challenging for newcomers. Genre-specific knowledge helps writers control how they use a genre. Knowledge of genre form is certainly an important focus of L2 writing instruction, but other areas of genre knowledge are also essential for manipulating genres to achieve our aims in a given context. Viewing genre knowledge as including multiple knowledge domains also gives teachers a framework for considering *what to teach* when teaching genre.

APPLICATION ACTIVITY

Think about a genre that you use regularly and believe that you can use fairly effectively. Make a list of what you know about this genre. Consider formal, rhetorical, process, and subject-matter knowledge. Next, consider a genre that you are relatively unfamiliar with and list what you know about that genre. How does your genre knowledge compare across these two genres?

Genre Awareness

While genre-specific knowledge refers to a user's understanding of a particular genre, genre awareness is broader. Devitt (2009) describes genre awareness as "a conscious attention to genres and their potential influences on people and the ability to consider acting differently within genres" (p. 347). It can be considered a kind of metacognitive knowledge, or "the explicit understanding of specific genres and of genre as a concept" (Gentil, 2011, p. 10). Cheng (2018) also includes in genre awareness the understanding of genre analysis as a conceptual framework for guiding students' exploration of genre samples. This metacognitive knowledge can help writers understand how genres (in general) function in relation to the people who use them and the contexts in which they are used.

Genre awareness can also contribute to genre-specific knowledge. For example, when I wrote my book endorsement blurb, I drew on my broader understanding of how writing works within various settings, and I used—informally—a framework for analyzing genres to help familiarize me with the book endorsement genre. In fact, both the first and second time I was asked to write a book endorsement, I pulled several books off my shelves and looked at their blurbs, comparing the similarities and differences.

Genre awareness may seem a little fuzzy as a concept. Because it is broader than genre-specific knowledge, it is (in theory) usable by writers in any genre situation. As a kind of metacognitive knowledge, it helps us understand what we already know that might be relevant to a current situation, and it can help us identify what we need to learn about a new genre. Genre awareness is important because it helps us approach unfamiliar genres or familiar genres in new rhetorical situations. Johns (2008) sees genre awareness as an important tool in helping students develop rhetorical flexibility, adapting "their socio-cognitive knowledge to ever-evolving contexts" (p. 239).

Connecting Genre-Specific Knowledge and Genre Awareness

So far, we've described genre knowledge and genre awareness separately, though they are clearly closely related and constitute our genre knowledge. One way to envision this relationship is through concentric circles, as shown in Figure 2.1. Within our genre awareness, we have knowledge of multiple specific genres. Genre awareness thus informs our genre-specific knowledge, which is also part of our broader genre awareness.

Some discussions of genre-based teaching distinguish between teaching for genre(-specific) knowledge and teaching for genre awareness (e.g., Russell & Fisher, 2009). Emphasizing one of these areas more than another makes sense on some level. In a class on dissertation writing, for example, students

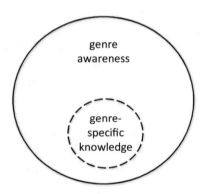

Figure 2.1 Genre Knowledge

will certainly need—and want—to develop their specific knowledge of dissertations. In a general composition course—like those often taught in secondary schools, intensive English programs, or early undergraduate writing classes—knowledge of specific genres may be less important (or practical) than developing broader awareness.

At the same time, a shift in emphasis does not mean that one kind of knowledge is irrelevant to instruction. Instead, research of student genre learning suggests that *both* areas of genre knowledge can inform each other, and they each have a valuable role to play in genre learning (e.g., Cheng, 2018; Yasuda, 2011). For this reason, Figure 2.1 depicts a porous boundary between the two areas.

As L2 writing teachers, our goals should be to help students build their genre-specific knowledge *and* their metacognitive genre awareness, since both will ultimately support them to be rhetorically flexible writers.

Principles of Genre-Based Writing Instruction

Genre-based writing instruction begins with the assumption that writing is shaped by its social groups, intended actions, and settings—all of which lead to the development of genres. Therefore, writing involves identifying and responding to the unique demands of a given situation. Genre-based pedagogy is essentially an approach to teaching that provides students with tools for understanding texts as genres, for analyzing those genres, and for using this insight in their writing.

There is no single method or technique in genre-based pedagogy; instead, it is characterized by several principles of writing, learning, and teaching.

1. **Writing is flexible, goal- or action-driven, and linked to social contexts and communities.**

   At the heart of genre-based pedagogy is the concept of genre. As we explored in the previous section, understanding texts as genres highlights the ways in which texts respond to the needs of particular communities and activities. Over time, repeated responses begin to converge, adopting common forms, practices, and rhetorical strategies. In other words, people start to develop shared preferences for responding to a situation and, eventually, those shared preferences are identified as genres.

   Understanding writing through the lens of genre helps us see it as flexible, goal- or action-driven, and linked to social contexts and communities. Genres are very different from formulaic structures or templates, such as five-paragraph essays. Genres also rarely have hard-and-fast rules (such as "Never use the passive voice"). Instead, genre examples share common conventions but also display variation. Some genres tolerate wider variation than others.

2. **Students should read, write, and explore relevant genres.** The range of genres in which students will write varies, sometimes considerably, depending on their educational or professional context. For students in elementary school, narratives, book reports, or science reports may be very common. In contrast, an engineer working at a global company may write mostly technical reports. In a genre-based writing classroom, a teacher typically focuses on genres that are most relevant and valuable to students. When exploring immediately relevant genres, students are more likely to encounter them outside of the classroom, possibly concurrently, or at least within a short space of time. Reducing the space and time between genres explored in a writing classroom and those used outside of the writing classroom may facilitate learning, particularly if students perceive similarities across tasks (James, 2008). This is not to suggest, however, that genre-based instruction should only focus on those genres that students will read and write in their immediate future. Exploration of any kind of genre can be beneficial to students because it engages them with the general concept of genre and can raise their broader genre awareness. Caplan and Farling (2016), for example, describe a unit in a university IEP in which students explore review genres, analyzing and composing product or restaurant reviews. Of course, students may write such reviews outside of class, but they will probably not need to do so in a university course. Still, by analyzing and composing reviews, they are developing their understanding of genre (as a concept), gaining practice in analyzing genres, and building a repertoire of genre-specific knowledge that can potentially be adapted to future related writing. For example, if students are later asked to write a review of a film viewed in a Russian history class, they can draw on and adapt some of what they have learned about review genres in their English class.

Relevance should be seen as a guiding principle rather than a hard-and-fast rule. Not every genre in the class needs to be immediately relevant to students, but, in general, most of the genres that are explored and composed in a class should have some relation to the students' goals and the goals of instruction.

3. **Awareness-raising sensitizes students to the conventions of genres and their rhetorical effects.**

Our discussions of genre and relevance have already hinted at the centrality of awareness-raising to genre-based pedagogy. Awareness-raising is what distinguishes genre-based pedagogy from simply "teaching genres." Swales (1990) referred to it as "rhetorical consciousness-raising," described as "sensitizing students to rhetorical effects, and to the rhetorical structures that tend to recur in genre-specific texts" (p. 213). In this way, genre-based instruction is similar to language awareness approaches or data-driven learning approaches that foreground the role of consciousness-raising derived through inductive exploration of language use.

Importantly, awareness-raising doesn't just help students build an understanding of a genre's forms and effects; it can also give them valuable insight into the communities that develop and use genres. In the case of advanced academic or professional writers, awareness-raising might lead to greater understanding of a community's values for knowledge production, or social practices for accomplishing particular aims.

4. **Student-driven exploration of genres deepens their rhetorical consciousness (or genre awareness).**

Student-driven exploration is the main vehicle for developing the kind of rhetorical consciousness that is a goal of genre-based teaching. Genre-based classrooms rely heavily on inductive learning in which students—with guidance from the instructor—explore texts, including the patterns and choices that authors make in different contexts and the rhetorical effects of those choices. Cheng (2018) describes the common goal of student explorations to be "making sense of how recurring genre-specific textual features may have certain rhetorical effects on them as readers and writers" (p. 32).

Student exploration may take many forms, though these are broadly referred to as **genre analysis tasks**. Because the goal of such tasks is rhetorical consciousness or awareness, genre analysis often focuses on "interactions between social situations and texts" (Cheng, 2018, p. 39). Genre analysis may therefore focus on very specific features of a genre (such as patterns and variations in writers' use of *I*), or on a constellation of features common to the genre.

Student exploration (rather than teacher presentation of genre features) is essential because it engages students directly in the practice of identifying patterns, learning a metacognitive strategy that they can use repeatedly as a writer. As students repeatedly analyze texts, they develop some metalanguage for talking about texts, and they learn new ways to look at writing and the choices that writers make.

5. Scaffolding instruction helps to make the complexity of genres more approachable.

Despite the emphasis on student exploration, teachers play an important role in genre-based approaches. One important role for teachers is to scaffold learning, making complex tasks manageable and supporting students' development of genre knowledge through guided, carefully sequenced tasks.

One example of scaffolding is found in the modeling and discussion of genre-texts. Because most students are not familiar with looking at and talking about texts as genres, teachers are important models. In the teaching/learning cycle, described in systemic functional linguistics (SFL) genre approaches, teachers model genre analysis, then guide joint-production of a text in the genre; finally, students practice composing their own texts (Hyland, 2007).

Scaffolding is also a consideration in sequencing tasks, as teachers may increase the challenge or complexity of genre analysis over time. Alternatively, scaffolding may relate to the dimensions of genre knowledge that students explore. For example, early in a course, teachers may wish to focus on analysis of lexico-grammatical features, then slowly introduce rhetorical moves analysis, and finally begin to connect those features to social practices or community values. Because there are so many aspects of genre to explore, scaffolding can help keep tasks manageable, so that students gradually build knowledge rather than quickly becoming confused or overwhelmed.

Finally, teachers may scaffold learning in terms of which genres students explore. In what she describes as a "socioliterate approach" to teaching, Johns (1997) introduces students to the concept and exploration of genre by focusing on familiar genres that they use in their everyday lives. As they become more comfortable as researchers of literacy practices, they gradually begin exploring less familiar genres, including those required of them in academic settings.

3. Designing Genre-Based Writing Tasks

Swales (1990) described **task** as central to genre-based instruction—it is through tasks that students explore genres, leading to the goal of awareness-raising. The importance of tasks is illustrated perhaps most clearly through Swales' and Feak's (e.g., 2011, 2012; Feak & Swales, 2009) genre-based text-books for graduate student writers, which make minimal use of explanations and instead engage students in numerous, well-sequenced explorations of writing and writing practices.

Designing genre exploration tasks can be time-consuming for teachers, but a few guidelines can aid in the process. This chapter describes six areas of task design: (1) selecting genres of focus, (2) sequencing and scaffolding tasks, (3) selecting sample texts, (4) keeping it student-centered, (5) context-ualizing tasks, and (6) producing genres.

Selecting Genres of Focus

One of the first decisions that teachers need to make is *which genres* students should explore. For writing classes that focus on specific genres—such as a class on thesis writing or proposal writing—this decision is fairly straight-forward. In more general writing classes, especially those in which teachers have autonomy in developing course content, selecting genres can be more challenging.

One approach is to focus on one or two broad categories of genre (such as argument or narrative) and engage students with several more specific genres within those categories. For example, a class focused on self-presentational genres could include exploration of memoirs, social media profiles, profes-sional websites, author bios, personal statements (university application essays), and job application letters. A class focused on persuasive genres could explore op-ed pieces, petitions, position papers, infographics, and TED talks. A class centered around source-based writing might engage stu-dents with genres like summaries, critiques, annotated bibliographies, white papers, and literature reviews.

Yasuda (2011) shares an example of a class focused on email writing, in which students explored 13 different email genres, such as apology emails, congratulation emails, request emails, reservation emails, and job application emails. In a class with more of a wide-angle approach to genre (Hyon, 2018), students may explore genres as diverse as everyday texts, professional faculty genres, and pedagogical genres (see Johns, 1997).

In discipline-oriented writing instruction, genres can reflect common disciplinary tasks and practices. Alternatively (or additionally), instruction might include non-discipline specific genres that help students explore subject-matter content. For example, in a history class focused on World War II, students could use their course content knowledge to write personal letters between soldiers and their families. In a psychology class in which students read psychology experiments, they could write press releases of studies that they read.

In sum, the selection of genres should consider course goals and student needs. Exploring a range of genres engages students with the ways in which genres respond to and are shaped by their rhetorical contexts. At the same time, there is some benefit to restricting the range enough so that students can draw on knowledge of one genre when exploring another, thus building a repertoire of genre knowledge that can also contribute to their metacognitive genre awareness.

Sequencing and Scaffolding Tasks

Once teachers have determined which genres to focus on, they can start to map out a general sequence of genres, along with a plan for introducing and building on various tools for analysis.

Teachers can choose from different principles in determining sequencing. One option is to sequence genres by topics—for example, moving from concrete and familiar topics (and their genres) toward more theoretical or unfamiliar ones (Hyland, 2004). Similarly, a course's genres may be sequenced in terms of genre families. For example, genre families could include procedures, information texts, or story texts. Within the genre family of procedures, students could explore instructions, procedures, and protocols (Hyland, 2004).

Another alternative is to sequence genres in terms of sets or chains (Hyland, 2004). For instance, a writing course for graduating Master's students might be sequenced around the genres of professional self-presentation, such as CVs, professional websites, job application letters, and portfolios.

In addition to sequencing genres, teachers will want to consider the sequencing of tasks. One suggestion is to gradually add to existing analysis tools, so that students gain repeated practice, but also develop more sophisticated genre awareness over time. In a course where the primary goal is genre awareness, teachers might pay special attention to task sequencing, adding increasingly social and critical elements of analysis. For instance, I used to teach an advanced undergraduate course to English majors in which a primary goal was to learn about genre. In this course, students selected one genre to explore, carrying out the following tasks over a 10-week term: analyzing the rhetorical situation, analyzing rhetorical moves, analyzing lexico-grammatical features, creating a genre prototype, interviewing a genre expert, adapting a prototype, analyzing a genre network, bending a genre, critiquing a genre, and creating a genre parody (Tardy, 2016).

The next sections in this chapter will provide numerous examples of genre features that students can analyze, as well as tools for analyzing them. It is unlikely that anyone could explore all of these features in any given class. Instead, prioritize a few and revisit and expand upon them throughout the term.

Selecting Sample Texts

One of the most time-consuming parts of genre-based writing instruction is locating sample texts. Samples can be used in their entirety or in excerpts for exploratory tasks. Ideally, you will want to find authentic texts that resemble a reasonable target for students and that demonstrate the variation inherent to genre.

Fortunately, internet technology can greatly ease the challenge of locating sample texts. Many non-academic texts can be found through simple web searches. Professional academic writing can be located online through applications like Google Scholar or library research databases.

Writing classes often focus on genres that are typically assigned in academic settings. Teachers may find themselves searching through former students' writing to locate examples and then needing to track down those students to gain permission to use their texts in class. Previous students' texts are an excellent source of samples, though they are not always available to teachers.

Online corpora of student writing might provide a useful source for many genres. The Michigan Corpus of Upper-level Student Papers (MICUSP) (http://micusp.elicorpora.info/) includes more than 800 student papers that received an A, written by upper-level undergraduates and graduate students (L1 and L2 English) across a range of disciplines at University of Michigan. Papers are classified into seven types: argumentative essays, creative writing, critiques/evaluations, proposals, reports, research papers, and response papers. Another alternative is CROW (https://crow.corporaproject.org/), a corpus and repository of writing that includes L2 English writing by early undergraduates in the U.S.

A strategy that should not be overlooked is to gradually build up your own "genre bank," or collections of samples that exemplify both prototypical and decidedly unconventional versions of genres. Personally, I have a file cabinet drawer, an email folder, and a digital folder all filled with genre samples that I encounter and think might, at some point, be fun and useful to bring into a classroom. Over time, your own genre banks can serve as an excellent teaching resource!

As a general rule of thumb, the texts that we use in designing exploratory tasks should be accessible to students; provide a range of variation, so that students see the flexibility of genre and the choices writers make; and engage students in some way. Of course, in practice, locating the "perfect" text can be a real challenge! Swales (2009) describes a common teacher dilemma in this way:

> One text may have the looked-for rhetorical structure and linguistic exemplification, but the content is too obscure and too unmanageable; another has attractive and utilizable content, but the structure is wrong or the treatment is too journalistic (Myers, 1990); and a third looks promising but it is too cluttered with intertextual links, asides and references to be useable "as is."
>
> (Swales, 2009, p. 5)

Although it is preferable to use unaltered texts as much as possible (exposing students to the real-life idiosyncrasies and complexities of writing), Swales (2009) notes that "*occasional* invocation of the...practitioners' creative powers" (p. 12)—altering or even constructing texts in realistic ways—may be helpful in task creation.

APPLICATION ACTIVITY

Identify a genre that you would like to have your students explore. Using some of the strategies described, locate at least three sample texts of this genre.

- *What difficulties did you have (if any) in locating texts?*
- *How similar are the rhetorical contexts in which each text was produced?*
- *Were you able to locate a set of texts that illustrate the genre's conventions as well as variations?*
- *Could you use these texts "as is" with your students, or would you need to adopt some creative license?*

Keeping It Student-Centered

It can be tempting to analyze genres for students, and many textbooks do this. It is not uncommon for textbooks to share a sample genre text and then label its parts for students. This approach does give students direct guidance, but it runs the risk of simplifying the variation of genre and suggesting a stronger stability to genres than they really have.

Rather than asking students to "learn" the labels for parts of genres, a genre-based approach engages students in discovering (themselves) the common ways to structure genres and the variations that exist. In this way, students explore various choices and their effects rather than learn a single set of conventions.

Contextualizing Analysis Tasks

Genre-based instruction essentially engages students in the work of a discourse analyst. Most students, however, do not see themselves as linguists or analysts, and they may, understandably, be less than enthusiastic about taking on this role. One strategy that John Swales and Christine Feak adopt in their textbooks is to contextualize analysis tasks in meaningful and fun ways. Here are some examples:

> *Example 1*
> Here is a typical CV written by an American citizen in 2010 to a U.S. audience. What do you like and dislike about it? What suggestions might you make to Robin Lee [the author]?
>
> (Swales & Feak, 2011, p. 87)[1]

> *Example 2*
> ...here is a draft email message that a graduate student, Akiko, plans to send to her advisor, Caroline Kelly. The email relates to the first version of the second chapter of her dissertation. The student shows the draft of this email message to the three other members of her study group for comments because she is worried that she may not be making a good impression. Their comments follow. Whom do you agree with and why?
>
> (Swales & Feak, 2009, p. 21)[2]

By giving students *reasons* for analyzing genres, we may raise their interest and engagement in classroom tasks. Similarly, by creating classroom tasks that are realistic, including situations students can imagine participating in, they are more likely to see the value in and relevance of the classroom activities to their writing.

Importantly, by adding contextual information to an analysis, we can directly engage students with the ways in which genres respond to specific rhetorical situations. Imaginary scenarios allow students to consider how the content or relationships between readers and writers, or the stakes involved in a particular text, might impact a writers' choices or readers' reactions to those choices.

APPLICATION ACTIVITY

How could you contextualize the following task for a genre and student population you work with? Write out a new version of this task that offers a more specific context for your students in comparing the three text samples.

Original Task: *Look at 3–5 samples of (Genre X). What are three ways in which these samples are similar? What are three ways in which they are different?*

---

1 Used with permission of University of Michigan Press.
2 Used with permission of University of Michigan Press.

Producing Genres

Awareness-raising analysis tasks are a central pillar of genre-based writing instruction, but a focus on analysis does not mean there is no role for text *production*. In fact, producing texts can be just as illuminating to students as analyzing them. Through production, writers are pushed to apply or adapt what they have learned about genres in exploratory tasks. Production of genre texts gives them opportunity to wrestle with variation and to make choices in their writing, whether those choices be about content, rhetorical moves, or linguistic features. Finally, through production, students may become more aware of how their own texts differ from other samples, in essence "noticing" gaps between texts they have read and those they are able to produce (Swain, 1993). Because it can engage metacognitive reflection (especially if prompted by teachers), text production can play a role in building students' knowledge of specific genres as well as their broader genre awareness.

To prepare students in producing genre texts, and to contribute to their genre awareness, teachers might use metacognitive scaffolds (Negretti & McGrath, 2018) like these:

Before Writing

- Students list the most common conventions of a genre and variations.
- Students describe the rhetorical context for which they will write (see Negretti & McGrath, 2018).
- Students annotate a sample text, noting features they especially like and those they don't like or might want to avoid.
- Students create a concept map of features of genre they will produce (see Wette, 2017).

After Writing

- Students annotate their own texts, noting choices that they made and briefly explaining why they made those choices (see Cheng, 2018).
- Students write a few sentences reflecting on the strengths of their writing and questions they have about specific rhetorical or linguistic choices they made.

Another approach to producing genre-texts, mentioned earlier, is to follow the teaching/learning cycle (TLC): deconstruction, joint construction, and independent construction (Rose & Martin, 2012). First, as a class, students analyze typical features of the genre, then they collaboratively produce a text in the genre, and finally they produce a text on their own in the genre. The "joint construction" phrase can be particularly illuminating for students, as the teacher guides the students and models the process of making choices in text production (see Caplan & Farling, 2016).

Text production can also take many other forms. Students might revise an existing text, perhaps writing it for a new rhetorical context or improving a weak text. Alternatively, they might finish an incomplete text or add new parts to an existing text. Student-produced texts may also include mimicking prototypical examples, using less conventional choices, writing parodies of a genre, or even writing poor examples of a genre (and explaining why the text would be unsuccessful). Ideally, teachers will engage students in all of these production tasks over the range of a course, giving them opportunities to play with genres rather than simply reproducing texts in formulaic ways.

4. Exploring Genre Form and Content in the Classroom

Examples of a genre share resemblances. As genre users, we often notice similarities in form and content intuitively, but we may not have the language to describe those similarities, or the tools to closely examine them. Genre analysis offers concrete strategies for students and teachers to explore genres systematically across a range of features. Through such analysis, students can gain a heightened awareness of the conventions and variations of a particular genre, while also learning strategies that they can use when encountering new genres. Strategies for exploring genre form and content are discussed next.

Rhetorical Moves

Rhetorical moves are, most simply, parts of a text. Crucially, those "parts" are defined by their rhetorical aim and are not necessarily marked in any way, such as by paragraphs or headings. For example, read this online reader review of the book *Americanah* by Chimamanda Ngozi Adichie.

> *I LOVED that book and I will buy anything this author writes. It described of course the racial tension and all the things Black Americans have to endure but this book is not limited to a Black readership but to the many people who settle in this country. I myself remember the huge surprise entering supermarkets which carry an inimaginable vast variety of yogurts and cereals. I also—like the author—wondered why toddlers in America were asked what they wanted to eat instead of just putting their mother's choice in front of them. The book is full of these details. The author's writing is not only serious and well written but it is also full of funny anecdotes. I warmly recommend it.*

Can you identify any shifts in rhetorical aim within this paragraph? Here is one possible way to categorize the rhetorical moves of this review:

> *I LOVED that book and I will buy anything this author writes.* [Provide a general assessment]

It described of course the racial tension and all the things Black Americans have to endure but this book is not limited to a Black readership but to the many people who settle in this country. [Describe book content or plot]

I myself remember the huge surprise entering supermarkets which carry an unimaginable vast variety of yogurts and cereals. I also—like the author—wondered why toddlers in America were asked what they wanted to eat instead of just putting their mother's choice in front of them. The book is full of these details. [Share personal connection to the book]

The author's writing is not only serious and well written but it is also full of funny anecdotes. [Describe strengths of the book]

I warmly recommend it. [Provide a recommendation]

You may have identified other moves or labeled your moves in slightly different ways. That is fine! When analyzing texts' rhetorical structure, there is no single correct "answer." Instead, the goal is to understand what the author is trying to do in the text and how they are doing that.

After looking at moves in one text, the next step is to look at more texts in this genre to see if they use similar or different moves. Are these moves typical to the genre? One more consumer book review is also provided; this time for the book *Pachinko* by Min Jin Lee. Can you identify the same moves in it as well? Are there any additional or different moves?

- Move 1: Provide a general assessment.
- Move 2: Describe book content or plot.
- Move 3: Share personal connection to the book.
- Move 4: Describe strengths of the book.
- Move 5: Provide a recommendation.

Review:

Best book of 2017 for me. because this novel explained a lots of things that I've always wondered but not to talk/ask questions growing up in Japan. I had some foreigner friends who was hiding their nationalities and change names to Japanese names, hearing pachinko places are not good places, some Korean friends gave me advice if I ever go to Korea, I should tell them I'm from Okinawa, (Not to say Japanese because older Koreans don't have good feeling about Japanese people) etc. well done with incorporating Japanese and Korean histories in the story. I was so attached to all the characters and stories of 4 generations of Korean family who lived in Japan. Defiantly recommend to my friends and great for book club. can't wait for next book of Min Jin Lee.

Although genres are marked by resemblances across texts, it is important to remember that they often allow for quite a bit of variation. The more reader reviews we look at, the more we might find ourselves modifying our original move categories and labels. We will also start to see which moves tend to be required (or "obligatory") in the genre, which are optional, and which might be very rare. Moves analysis should not be presented to students as an exact science, but as one interpretive approach to understanding discourse structure.

Initially, students may confuse rhetorical moves with "parts" of texts that they have been taught, such as "introduction," "body," and "conclusion." It is useful to explain that those categories tend to be broader than rhetorical moves. For example, we can identify moves that are common *within* an introduction or conclusion. It can also be helpful to have students use verbs—rather than nouns—when labeling the rhetorical moves that they identify. Using verbs can help them focus on what the move is trying to *do*.

Identifying common rhetorical moves can be extremely helpful for student-writers because it gives them a way to think about text structure that is grounded in the text's rhetorical aims. Therefore, identifying moves can help students think about the goals that they want to achieve in their text and how they can achieve them.

There are many ways to introduce rhetorical moves analysis to students. It can be useful to start with very short, familiar texts. Genres like birthday cards, wedding invitations, or online consumer restaurant reviews are all generally accessible and somewhat familiar to students, depending on their ages and backgrounds. Short academic texts like abstracts, problem statements, or summaries can also be useful for introducing and practicing moves analysis.

While researchers use a fairly detailed process for moves analysis (see Hyon, 2018, pp. 33–35), a more streamlined process is usually sufficient for classroom analysis:

A. Collect a relevant set of texts in the genre.
B. Gain a sense of the genre's audience(s) and purpose(s).
C. Establish a working set of moves.
D. Identify patterns in move frequency and sequencing across the texts.
E. Consider the reasons for and effects of different patterns of moves.

It is especially important for students to consider *why* these move patterns exists, as prompted by Steps B and C. Why would authors choose to include these moves or to sequence the moves in these ways? Why do some authors choose *not* to use certain moves? In what situations might some moves be more or less necessary? What are the potential effects of different choices that authors make with rhetorical moves?

As an example, think back to the moves tentatively identified in the online book reviews:

- Move 1: Provide a general assessment.
- Move 2: Describe book content or plot.
- Move 3: Share personal connection to the book.
- Move 4: Describe strengths of the book.
- Move 5: Provide a recommendation.

Students might consider how each move helps the writer carry out their goals in writing the review. Some of these moves (such as Move 1) are obligatory: people read book reviews to know what others thought about the book, so a book review must include some kind of assessment to satisfy readers' needs. Other moves (such as Move 3) are optional. Part of our assessment of a book is often related to our personal experiences or connections to it, so it makes sense that reviewers often include this information in a review. However, including personal experience is not required to carry out the aim of a book review, and many reviews do not use this move.

When students are comfortable using moves analysis to explore genres, they can begin to apply it to more challenging and less familiar texts. As they broaden out to examine longer texts or genres with wider variation, they will find it especially useful to compare their analyses with their classmates'.

Through moves analysis, students might also analyze how the same genres are used by different communities. For example, they can compare methodology sections of research papers in social science fields versus hard sciences, or in studies that include human participants versus non-human laboratory experiments. Comparing genre moves across communities helps students contextualize rhetorical moves even more. Studies with human participants (especially ethnographic studies), for example, often include a move in which the researcher describes their positionality and how it impacted the study. This move reflects a value of social constructionism in some social science research, demonstrating a belief that such research can never be truly "objective," and that the researcher's own subject position plays a role in the research and interpretation of the data. This move is not present in all social science research, and it is almost never found in laboratory experiments.

Rhetorical moves can be explored in the classroom in numerous ways; it is not always necessary to do a formal moves analysis. Some other activities that help students explore rhetorical move more implicitly are listed:

- *Jigsaw texts*: Break up and jumble a text by moves and ask students to put the parts back into what they think is the original order (Hyon,

2018; Swales, 1990). Compare across groups and ask students to explain their rationale for different choices. This activity can be used to introduce a new genre and its moves, or it could be used to review a moves pattern that students have already uncovered. Jigsawing texts like this can be especially interesting because there is often more than one effective way to re-sequence a text; students can discuss the effects of different sequencing choices.

- *Identifying missing rhetorical moves*: After students have explored common moves within a genre, give them a sample text that omits a very common or even obligatory move. They can work individually or in pairs to identify which move is missing, and to consider how omitting that move changes the text. Does the text still achieve its aim? How might it be perceived differently by readers with or without this move?
- *Evaluating texts with different rhetorical moves*: Students can be given a set of three or four sample texts in a genre. These samples should include some variation in rhetorical moves; for example, the texts may include and omit slightly different moves, they may include moves in different sequences, or the same move may be much longer or shorter in different texts. Students can compare the various approaches and rank-order the texts in terms of which they think would be most effective in a given context. The discussion of their rankings highlights the various rhetorical effects of different writing choices and may touch on the important role of context in shaping these effects.

Linguistic Features

As readers, we often intuitively sense that genres vary in their linguistic choices. For example, when asked about the language use in a text such as a research article, students are likely to point out that it uses "formal" language. When pressed to explain what makes it formal, however, many students struggle to identify specific features.

One strength of genre-based instruction is that it gives students simple tools (and some metalanguage) for understanding the language of texts and genres. Thinking about texts and language in this way can raise our awareness of *why* certain texts "look" different from others and can help us think more consciously about the linguistic choices we make in our writing across genres.

There are numerous ways to analyze linguistic features of genres. Three areas are discussed: grammatical features, lexical features, and lexico-grammatical features. While these categories may be useful for teachers in considering different aspects of language to focus on, they are not very important or meaningful for students. Instead, all of these areas can be presented to students as falling broadly within the category of "language features."

Grammatical Features

Students (and many teachers) often associate grammar with error or accuracy. Many second language students have taken classes focused on grammar rules and have taken exams that expect error-free writing. Discussing grammar in relation to genre is a bit different.

Instead of focusing on grammar rules, genre-based activities help students explore grammatical *choices* within texts. As with moves analysis, students can learn to identify common choices (or conventions) within a genre to gain a sense of how writers typically write in this genre and what kind of variations might be found. The focus is on grammatical conventions and the reasons for those conventions rather than on accuracy or error.

To illustrate this quickly, look at the following customer reviews of the Bread & Butter Café in Tucson, Arizona:

Review #1
Mostly Friendly diner Breakfast and Lunch crowd.
Reasonable prices and large variety. Eat here if you are in the area.

Review #2
My favorite place for breakfast staff knows my daughter since she was little they give hugs all around. Great service great food love it love it love it.

Review #3
Friendly staff. And good comfort food! Stumbled across this by accident.
Don't judge this place from the outside.

You may notice that these reviews (which are typical of this genre) share several grammatical conventions. First, they all include sentences that omit the subject and/or verb. In the examples, the missing subjects and verbs are included in brackets:

- *[The restaurant has] Reasonable prices and large variety.* (Review #1)
- *[The restaurant had] Great service great food love it love it love it.*
  (Review #2)
- *[I] Stumbled across this by accident.* (Review #3)

Students may have learned that these grammatical forms can be called "sentence fragments" because they are missing required elements of a sentence. In most academic writing, students learn to avoid sentence fragments. However, sentence fragments are very common in online reviews because the reviews are usually written quickly (often on a mobile phone) and very informally. Omitting unnecessary elements makes it easier for the writer to type a review on a small screen. It is also notable that sentence fragments are very common in spoken conversation, and their use here contributes to the informality and interpersonal nature of the review. There is no "grade" attached to an online review; the goal instead is to communicate an evaluation of the product or service to other potential customers.

When people read online reviews, they also read quickly (again, often on a mobile phone), so they want short reviews in which key information is easy to find. Sentence fragments allow writers to highlight that key information. However, while *most* reviews make frequent use of sentence fragments, not all do. Here is an example of another review for the Bread & Butter Café; this review uses only complete sentences:

> Review #4
> *This is my joint. It's in a humble and honest setting. It's simple and to the point. The food is what brings the crowds in. It's crowded, but there is a reason why so many people come to eat here. I always go in and get the chicken fried steak special and it keeps me coming back. The hash browns are cooked crispy brown but soft. I just can't get enough of this place.*

This example helps demonstrate that writers still have options and that sentence fragments are not required in this particular genre.

As an analyst, I also wondered whether sentence fragments might be less common in reviews for a more formal dining establishment, so I looked at reviews for Café Poca Cosa, an upscale Sonoran Mexican restaurant in Tucson. Again, I found that nearly every review included at least one sentence fragment.

Suspecting that this grammatical feature might be tied to the informality of the crowd-sourced reviews online, I looked through some restaurant reviews in *The New York Times*, a national newspaper with a notable restaurant review section. I found numerous examples of sentences beginning with *And* or *But* (a somewhat colloquial form), but I found no examples of the omitted subjects and verbs that are so frequent in the online customer reviews.

Why might sentence fragments be so common in online customer reviews but so rare (or even absent) in *The New York Times* restaurant reviews?

The rhetorical context of the reviews can help explain this distinction. Online restaurant reviews are written by customers with no required expertise in evaluating restaurants, while the *NYT* reviews are written by professional food critics. The *NYT* reviewers, therefore, are also establishing their credibility through their more formal (and also much more thorough and detailed) reviews. The use of formal sentence structure contributes to the more credible nature of the *NYT* reviews.

In addition, the online customer reviews are generally written very quickly and are not edited. Anyone can write a customer review on the website I examined (Yelp.com), and the reviews are posted as written. In contrast, *NYT* reviews are likely written over at least several hours (if not days), possibly with multiple drafts or at least revisions, and ultimately edited by a professional editor.

This short example of the use of one grammar feature—sentence fragments—illustrates how grammatical choices are intimately related to other rhetorical features of a genre. A challenge for teachers can be knowing *which* grammatical features to focus on in genre analysis activities. One strategy is to look for features that are especially common in the genre and that may also be somewhat unique. For example, the omission of the sentence subject is a very common grammatical convention in résumés or CVs in some countries, giving rise to forms such as:

- *Led an international team of product researchers*
- *Designed solutions for on-site support issues*

When teaching CV writing, then, subject omission would be an excellent language feature for students to explore.

Another strategy is to focus on grammatical features that students struggle with in a particular genre, such as, perhaps, verb tense. Some grammatical features that may be useful to examine, depending on the genre of focus and your students' experience and strengths, are provided:

Common Grammatical Features to Explore
- verb tense
- passive/active voice
- contractions
- nominalizations (i.e., nouns created from other parts of speech, such as participation, abstraction, or mechanization)
- omitted sentence subject or sentence fragments

- sentence types (e.g., statement/declarative, imperative, interrogative, exclamatory)
- sentence structures (e.g., simple, compound, complex, compound-complex)
- embedded clauses
- punctuation (e.g., exclamation points, semi-colons, colons, omission of punctuation)

When analyzing grammar features with students, it is important to connect grammatical choices to the genre's aims and rhetorical contexts. How do these language choices help fulfill the writers' goals? Why might they be common in this particular setting? It is also essential to illustrate the variation that can exist in grammatical features of a genre, helping students to see grammatical conventions as choices rather than rules.

APPLICATION ACTIVITY

Locate at least five book reviews from a reputable newspaper you are familiar with. The reviews should be written by a book critic (though they can each be written by a different critic). What is one grammatical feature that is commonly used in the samples? What is one grammatical feature that is rare (or never used) in the samples? Why do you think these conventions of use are found in the sample texts? Do you think you would find the same conventions in online consumer book reviews? Why or why not?

Lexical Features

In addition to grammatical features, many genres also have preferences for certain lexical features. For example, what do you notice about the underlined words and phrases in this excerpt from a research article abstract by Korsós and colleagues (2018)?

A total of forty, 7-week-old male rats were exposed to the 'rodentized' version (twice as fast as and one octave higher than the original) of Mozart's Sonata for Two Pianos in D major for 10 minutes a day for

10 weeks. One group (10 rats) received the musical <u>stimuli</u> before ('B'), another during ('D') and the third before and during ('BD') the memory test, while the ten control ('C') animals were kept in silence. The animals' <u>spatial learning</u> and <u>memory ability</u> was tested in an <u>8-arm radial maze</u>. Rats exposed to the music showed a significant (7.1%) improvement in <u>task acquisition</u> (Group BD), but it did not practically change in Group D and worsened by 10.5% in Group B. The <u>2-h working memory</u> significantly improved by 12.1% (BD) while practically did not change in Groups B and D. The <u>reference memory</u> improved by 11.9% in Group BD, but did not change in Group B and D, compared to the Control. The performance of the groups during the <u>4-h working memory test</u> did not differ significantly.

(Korsós et al., 2018, p. 94)

All of the underlined words might be considered specialized **jargon**—that is, they have a very specific meaning related to the research in animal behavior science and are unlikely to be familiar to lay people. Scientific, legal, professional, and technical texts often include extensive jargon. Jargon serves as a shorthand for insiders, making it easier to refer to common, complex ideas in fewer words; however, the use of jargon also can make texts confusing or even inaccessible to outsiders.

Jargon is a lexical feature that is common in certain genres, especially those written by and for highly specialized groups of people. It is relatively rare in genres written for wide audiences who have a range of background knowledge on the topic.

Which of the following genres do you think are likely to include a lot of jargon, which do you think include little or no jargon, and which are you unsure about?

- scientific posters for an undergraduate student science symposium
- history textbooks for elementary school
- national education policy documents
- corporate mission statements
- travel postcard notes

You could look up a few examples of these genres to confirm your answers, but based on what we know about the various audiences, a reasonable guess would be that the scientific posters and education policy documents would include the most jargon. Corporate mission statements may include some "corporate-ese," but are generally written for the public, so jargon is probably limited. History textbooks for elementary students are probably mostly jargon-free, and travel postcards likely include no professional jargon (though they may include "insider" words or phrases only understood by the writer and receiver).

As with grammatical features, classroom tasks will likely focus only on lexical features that are especially relevant to the genres students are exploring or those features that students find challenging. A list of some lexical features that may be useful to examine, depending on the genre of focus and students' experience and strengths, is given:

Common Lexical Features to Explore
• jargon
• slang
• formal/informal words
• abbreviations or acronyms
• latinate or other non-English words or phrases
• titles/naming conventions (e.g., Ms., Dr., no title)
• idioms

Lexico-Grammatical Features

A final category of linguistic features are *lexico-grammatical features*, a blend of the two categories we have already explored. Lexico-grammatical features bring together grammatical categories with specific lexical choices. For example, one common lexico-grammatical category is *hedges*. Hedges are words or phrases that are used to mitigate or qualify a statement, to make it more tentative. Some modal verbs (a grammatical category) are commonly used as hedges (e.g., *could, might, would*). Hedges also consist of other words that express qualification, including some adverbs (e.g., *apparently, slightly*), adjectives (e.g., *tentative, possible*), verbs (e.g., *seems, appears, suggests*).

There has been a good deal of formal research into lexico-grammatical features of different genres, especially in academic writing. Exploring lexico-grammatical patterns can be very illuminating for students, but it will be a new way of thinking about writing for many. For this reason, it can be helpful to limit the metalanguage used to analyze lexico-grammatical features. For example, they probably do not need to know the term *lexico-grammatical features*, though terms like *hedges* and *boosters* can be very helpful.

Preferences for lexico-grammatical features are often linked to a writer's rhetorical aims within a genre. Hedges, for example, are used to qualify claims, reflecting the writer as careful or cautious. Boosters, on the other hand, are used to make bold claims and may, therefore, be used in a highly persuasive text (e.g., an opinion editorial), or one in which a sense of urgency is being expressed (e.g., a petition).

One lexico-grammatical feature that students especially like to discuss is personal pronouns, such as the use of *I/me/my* or *we/us/our*. Many students have been told to avoid using personal pronouns in academic writing, though they may find, through genre analysis, that this "rule" is hardly stable or generalizable. Instead, genres have different preferences for pronoun use. Additionally, there is often variation in pronoun use across and even within communities of users. By comparing such variation, students can gain insight into how choices about pronoun use might affect the rhetorical nature of the text.

To illustrate such comparison, look at the following statements regarding the study of rats by Korsós and colleagues (2018). What are the differences in pronouns use? What effects do the different options have?

A. The control (C) group (10 rats/group) <u>was not exposed to</u> any music; they spent the same time in a 3rd room, but in silence.
B. <u>The researchers did not expose</u> the control (C) group (10 rats/group) to any music; they spent the same time in a 3rd room, but in silence.
C. <u>We did not expose</u> the control (C) group (10 rats/group) to any music; they spent the same time in a 3rd room, but in silence.
D. <u>I did not expose</u> the control (C) group (10 rats/group) to any music; they spent the same time in a 3rd room, but in silence.

This set of variations shows how writers can choose to foreground or background their own personal role in conducting research. While Sentence A completely masks the role of humans in carrying out the experiment, Sentence D, through the use of *I*, lays bare the individual researcher's action. The sentences each have a different rhetorical effect, and it is up to writers to select an option that they feel will be most effective in the context in which they are writing.

Lexico-grammatical features that are commonly explored in genre analysis, especially in academic writing, are listed. You will find different features to be more or less relevant for different genres and groups of students.

Common Lexico-Grammatical Features to Explore
• hedges (e.g., *apparently, appear, in general, may, not necessarily, tend, unclear*)
• boosters (e.g., *always, convincingly, determine, we find that, prove, unquestionable/ly*)
• evaluative adjectives (e.g., *complex, noteworthy, problematic, tenuous*)

- personal pronouns (e.g., *I/me/my, they/their, you/your*)
- metadiscourse (e.g., *In this article, we..., As noted previously..., A final point is...*)
- reporting verbs (e.g., *acknowledges, argues, maintains, notes, states*)

Classroom tasks for exploring linguistic features of genres can take many forms, but it is a good guideline to focus on just one or a small set of linguistic features in a single task. Here are a few examples:

- *Rank order texts*: Give students an excerpt or whole text within a particular genre, re-written in at least three different ways, each with minor linguistic changes like different pronoun use, different uses of jargon, or use of simplified through more complex sentences. Students compare the linguistic differences across the samples and then rank-order them in terms of which text they think would be the most through least successful in a given context of use.
- *Write an ineffective text*: Students can learn just as much by producing *poor* examples of a genre as they can by producing effective ones. After students have already explored a particular genre in some detail, including linguistic features, ask them to compose (individually or collaboratively) a genre-text that they feel would be *ineffective* in most contexts. Ask them to focus on linguistic features rather than design, content, or rhetorical moves.
- *Modifying stance*: Author stance (or attitude toward the content in the text) is partly expressed through linguistic features. To raise students' awareness of how stance may be revealed, ask them to write a genre such as an academic summary in three ways: one neutral, in which the author's opinion about the text is not revealed; one very positive, in which the author shows a positive attitude about the text being summarized; and one negative, in which the author's stance toward the summarized text is pessimistic or disapproving. This activity can also be done as a whole class, in which the class begins with a neutral summary and then works together, with the teacher's guidance, to make it more positive or negative.

Design and Multimodal Elements

So far, we have considered rhetorical moves and linguistic features of genres, both of which give rise to recognizable forms. As genre users, you are also surely aware that genre forms extend beyond those two areas. Some genres are recognizable simply by their page layout or design. Without too much difficulty, you can probably conjure an image of what the following genres generally *look like* on a page:

- a scientific journal article
- a job application letter
- a condolences card
- a text conversation between friends
- a university website

There will probably be differences in this design or formatting across communities of users and in different languages. In addition, some genres may be primarily or solely made up of words (e.g., a job application letter), some make some (but limited) use of multimodal features (e.g., the use of .gifs or emojis in text messages between friends), and still other genres integrate numerous modalities, including images, videos, charts, and varying uses of fonts and colors (e.g., a university website).

Although we tend to think of digital genres as being more multimodal than print genres, many print genres make extensive use of color, page layout, or images to communicate their ideas. Think, for example, of print newspapers, public posters announcing music events, or signs that people hold up at marches or protests.

Design and modality choices are important to most genres, so they are useful features for students to analyze. They can also be especially fun for L2 students to analyze as they do not rely on linguistic knowledge.

There are many different features of design or multimodality that can be explored. Students who are new to academic writing in a particular context, for example, might examine design conventions for an academic paper. They might notice features like margins, font preferences, title formatting, page numbers, headings, or paragraphing.

Common Design and Multimodal Features to Explore
- headings, titles
- page layout, white space
- color
- font
- emojis
- figures, tables, charts
- images
- audio
- video
- animation

APPLICATION ACTIVITY

Examine the homepage for the following organizations' websites: Doctors Without Borders (Médecins San Frontières), International Committee of the Red Cross and Red Crescent, UNICEF, and Oxfam.

In what ways does each homepage make use of multimodal elements? What kind of information is communicated through images, words, and videos? How do you think these choices help the organizations achieve their goals of informing the public of their work and persuading people to donate to their organization?

Ideas for classroom tasks that explore genre design and multimodality are provided.

- *Design a genre text*: When genres have complex designs, it is useful to have students simply explore that formatting without worrying about the text itself. For genres like résumés/CVs, presentation slides, poster displays, or brochures, begin by giving students the text to work with, and ask them to reformat it in an appropriate, or even "prototypical," way, based on their analysis of samples of the genre. When they have finished, they can compare how different students reformatted the same text, discussing the particular choices made and reasons for those choices.
- *Redesign a text:* Similar to the previous task, students can be given a poorly designed example of a genre and be asked to revise it, focusing on formatting and design. Groups can compare what they identified to be problematic in the original text and why, and then explain the changes that they made. The class can also vote on the most effective redesigned text.

Content

Common conventions for a genre's form play a big role in making texts recognizable as a particular genre. Somewhat related to form is the content or subject matter of a genre. For novice writers, it can be very helpful to understand what types of content are very common, somewhat common, or even rare or taboo within a particular genre.

Résumés or CVs offer good examples. By looking at sample résumés, students can gain a sense of what content is commonly included and what is less common or even avoided. These preferences, of course, vary by job type as well as geographic location. For example, information about one's marital status may be common in some countries, but is strongly discouraged in others.

The content conventions of a genre are related to rhetorical moves, but they can also be explored separately. Take, for instance, an academic book review. One required rhetorical move is to "Evaluate aspects of the book," but the *content* of evaluation is not specified by the move. Novice writers might look at sample book reviews—with the understanding that these vary by discipline or publication venue—to gain a better sense of what is common content for evaluating books, as well as variations. What aspects of books are evaluated, for example? Is the evaluation mostly positive, mostly negative, or a balance between the two? Analyzing these kinds of content preferences can be very useful for writers approaching an unfamiliar genre.

Students may also explore the background knowledge that a genre assumes readers have and the kinds of knowledge that cannot be assumed, depending on the rhetorical context. A cooking recipe in a children's cookbook, for instance, is likely to include very simple but specific details about cooking procedures, or even integrate photographs or images to illustrate what it means to "whip eggs into stiff peaks" or to "mix until just blended." Detailed explanations of these instructions are not common in cookbooks for advanced chefs.

Students can also explore content preferences in academic texts. For instance, how much detail is needed in a lab report? Which specialized terms require explanation in a literary analysis essay written for a class versus one published in an academic journal? Considerations of audience knowledge should guide such explorations.

One common convention in source-based academic writing is to include references to sources that the author is using. Genre scholars have explored citation patterns extensively, and they are a useful area for students to examine through classroom analysis tasks. (Feak and Swales (2009) provides excellent examples of citation analysis activities.)

Some citation practices are form-related (e.g., preferences for different documentation styles or for authors' names to be integrated into a sentence or relegated to a parenthetical citation or footnote), but other aspects are related to content. Writers in more advanced academic settings often need to learn which kinds of information should be cited and what can be considered "common knowledge," not requiring a citation. They should also be familiar with, in some cases, some of the key publications or scholars that are cited when writing on a specific topic.

This type of specialized content knowledge is gained over time and is not easy to analyze, though some exploration is possible in a classroom. In a class on thesis writing or writing for publication, students might explore texts in their specific area of interest and create a map of the key scholars or scholarly works. They can interview authors in the area (such as their advisors) to learn more about the politics of citing or not citing particular people or works. What are the implications of citing Scholar X but not Scholar Y in this area? There are no single answers to these kinds of questions, but focused exploration of them can raise writers' awareness of the intricacies of research writing and the various ways in which writers "stand on the shoulders of giants."

APPLICATION ACTIVITY

Locate 5–10 examples of a genre that is important to you as a teaching professional. For example, you may want to look at teaching philosophies, professional website profiles, or student feedback. Use some of the strategies in this section to analyze the genre's conventions for form and content. You may, for example, look at three or four features from these categories:

- *rhetorical moves*
- *grammar features*
- *lexical features*
- *lexico-grammatical features*
- *visual design*
- *format*
- *multimodality*
- *content*

Based on your analysis, what have you learned about common conventions of form or content in this genre? Why do you think these features are common? How does their use relate to the purpose, users, and context of the genre? What are some variations that you have identified across your samples? What might have influenced the different variations that you found?

5. Exploring Genre Practices in the Classroom

In language and writing instruction, we typically think of genres in terms of their form, often some kind of written text. But genres are really social practices that have become "typified" over time through repeated use and the development of social preferences. Previously, we discussed the example of a thank-you note to illustrate how genres are actually categories of social practices.

It is useful for students to understand writing (and written genres) as practices. Many students have been taught very rigid rules about writing (e.g., *Never use I in an academic paper*), or have learned to use static structures like five-paragraph essay templates. Re-focusing students' attention on the practices that are part of a genre can help them see genre forms as part of the choices that writers make as they respond to social situations.

There are many genre practices that students can explore, even in a writing classroom. This chapter will focus on three: genre uptake and networks, composing processes, and distributing or sharing genres.

Genre Uptake and Networks

Students may think of writing as happening in isolated tasks, written in response to an assignment and never to be returned to. In reality, even genres in educational settings are part of more complex intertextual webs, sometimes called **genre networks**.

Sometimes these networks are chronological, with one genre (or, more likely a set of genres) prompting a response (another genre or set of genres), which then leads to another response. For example, consider the genres involved in participating in an academic conference: conference call for papers→individual conference proposal→acceptance letter→program book→conference presentation. The ways in which genres often respond to a previous genre has been compared to the action in a tennis match (Freadman,

1987), with different players (or genre users) putting the ball back in one another's court with each turn they take.

When we think of genres in terms of responses, or **uptakes** (Bawarshi, 2003; Freadman, 1987), we can see more clearly how they relate to goal-oriented actions that communities carry out. Using a genre allows us to participate in some kind of activity within a community. If we choose our genres (and our genre forms) wisely, we are more likely to get a positive response from other participants.

Sometimes genres are part of fairly complex genre networks. Considering how a genre interacts with other genres (and their communities) can help identify both the near and far uses of a genre, such as how genres may become a part of a later action and how they are taken up for new activities. Additionally, looking at genres' networks can help us see how users draw upon multiple genres in order to carry out one genre. For instance, in some cases, genres may omit certain content because it is included in a separate—but linked—genre. A job application letter does not include every single detail of a person's work history because that information appears in a separate genre (the resume or CV). Similarly, a job application letter may draw explicitly or implicitly on the job advertisement to which it responded. An application letter also may be used in multiple activities: to apply for jobs (by applicants), to identify top candidates (by employers), to offer a point of reference during an interview (also by employers), and perhaps to identify an appropriate starting salary (by a human resources department or top-level employee).

By situating a genre within its larger network, students can begin to gain a sense of its role within a larger activity and by multiple users. They might ask: what does this genre do within the larger genre network? What does it *not* have to do? What other genres does it refer to or incorporate? What genres might later respond to this genre?

Here are some questions that can guide exploration of a genre's uptake and larger genre network:

- When is this genre used?
- Are there alternative genres that could be used in this situation? If so, how do writers choose the appropriate genre?
- What other genres are linked to this genre? How do the genres affect each other?
- Who writes the related genres? Who reads them?

APPLICATION ACTIVITY

A lesson plan is a common teaching genre, and it offers a good example of how genres exist within larger networks. Draw a visual map that illustrates some of the genres that commonly work together in relation to teacher lesson plans. You might want to look at a lesson plan you created recently and identify all of the other genres that you drew on in creating and teaching this lesson; these genres should all be included in your visual map, perhaps. Also try to include in your map other genres that might later draw on or reference your lesson plans. If possible, use arrows to indicate relationships between all of these genres.

Composing Processes

It is not uncommon for writing instructors to teach composing processes like planning, revising, and editing. A genre perspective also allows us to see how such processes are also affected by the genre itself. For each of the following genres, consider some of the ways in which their composing processes are different:

- a social media post to friends
- an email to a work supervisor requesting a schedule change
- a letter of complaint to a company
- a scientific report submitted for publication

You may have noticed that these genres have different audiences (friends, supervisors, unknown companies, reviewers and scientific researchers), may be written on different devices (mobile phone, computer), and have very different outcomes at stake. As such, it is not surprising that their composing processes differ too. A social media post may take just a few seconds to write, while a scientific report would likely take weeks or months. Some of these genres may be written independently, while others require consultation or collaboration. Some make use of other sources, such as photographs, schedule sheets, or even extensive scientific literature. In some cases, the writers may need to look at other examples of the genre or even follow explicit guidelines for writing in the genre.

Here are some questions that can guide exploration of a genre's composing processes:

- In what ways do people compose in this genre?
- How long does it typically take?
- What resources are often needed? Consider other texts, technology, people, etc.
- Are there any timing constraints for producing this genre? For example, does it need to be composed quickly? Does it need to be created shortly after a particular event or action, or before another event or action?

Distributing or Sharing Genres

Genres can vary widely in how they are distributed or shared with others, and these differences can have consequences for a genre's form as well. Consider, for example, the academic poster, including science fair posters, academic conference posters, or classroom project posters, to give a few examples. Because the poster is usually situated on a wall or easel, readers have to stand while reading it. In a crowded space, they may have to stand back a little bit, their view may be obscured, and they may or may not have a chance to ask the author questions about the poster's contents. All of these features of the genre's distribution impact the choices a writer makes when creating an academic poster. Writers often use headings to help guide readers through the poster, and they incorporate visuals to give information in formats that are easy to read quickly. Text is kept to a minimum and is usually in a large font. As this example shows, considering the ways in which a genre will be shared with its audience can help writers make effective choices in their texts.

A few of the questions that can guide exploration of a genre's distribution practices are:

- With whom is the genre distributed or shared?
- How is it distributed or shared? In what kind of space(s)?
- When is it distributed or shared? What are readers doing before or while using the genre?
- In what forms, media, or modes?

APPLICATION ACTIVITY

Imagine that your students are writing a historical timeline, highlighting key moments in a major historical event. They should use photographs and brief text in their timeline. How might their choices for their text's form change depending on the following distribution scenarios?

> a. *Create a poster of the timeline to be displayed in a poster session with visitors (parents, other teachers, or peers).*
> b. *Create a website of the timeline to be shared publicly.*
> c. *Create a timeline on paper to be submitted in print form to the teacher only.*

Classroom Exploration

There are numerous ways to incorporate exploration of genre practices into the classroom. The following activities provide some examples.

- *Prepare a pre-writing genre map*: Before writing in a genre, students create a visual map that illustrates all of the related genres and their communities. They can illustrate how related genres are sequenced or genres that are drawn on or incorporated into their target genre. They may also want to include information about the users of each genre in their map. After creating their map, students can write a short list of ways in which the genre network might affect the genre's form.
- *Interview a genre user about composing processes*: When encountering a new genre, students may not have a lot of information about its practices. In these cases, it can be very useful for students to interview experienced genre users about how they compose in the genre. Questions shared previously in this chapter can provide some guidance. If finding genre users is challenging for students, the instructor can bring a guest speaker (or two) to class for a group interview or panel discussion.

6. Exploring the Social and Rhetorical Aspects of Genre in the Classroom

As we've seen, genres arise out of social contexts and are shaped by social groups or communities. Therefore, writers can learn a lot about genres by understanding the contexts in which they occur and the communities that use them. In many ways, it is these social and rhetorical aspects of genre that are hardest to learn in a language or writing classroom. This section outlines suggestions for helping students to explore these social and rhetorical aspects of genre.

Rhetorical Situation

The term **rhetorical situation** is generally used to describe a situation in terms of the users (audience and author), goals or aims, and context. It is the *recurrence* or repetition of similar rhetorical situations that give rise to genres. As a situation happens again and again—not identically, but in relatively similar ways—people begin to find shared ways of responding to the situation. These responses are what we often refer to as genres.

Take, for example, the recurring situation of a wedding. When a wedding occurs, those involved often want to invite others to attend. Because it is an important life event, the invitation is more formal than a phone call or text message; wedding invitations are usually made on formal paper, though there are many variations today, including digital invitations.

Think back to some wedding invitations that you have seen or even produced—you can also locate many examples through an image search in a web browser. What do you know about the following features of the rhetorical situation for these invitations?

- Users
  - Who is the author (or authors) of the invitation? Are they created by a wedding planner or company?
  - Who is paying for the wedding?

- How formal is the wedding? How many guests?
- What are the cultural or linguistic backgrounds of the couple and the guests?
- How traditional or non-traditional are the couple?

• Goals
  - What is the primary goal of the wedding invitation? What is it used *to do*?
  - What might be some secondary goals?
  - Are there any "hidden agendas" at play?

• Context
  - What are some of the social values that surround weddings in different contexts?
  - In the case of this particular wedding, is the couple adhering to, bending, or violating social values in any way?
  - Where will the wedding be held? Will that influence who can attend?
  - What do you know about the couple's personal histories or other family details that might influence the wedding in some way?

As you think through these questions and others, also consider how these features of rhetorical situation influence how the wedding invitation is written and designed. For example, does the issue of who pays for the wedding have an effect on the invitation in any way? What about the formality of the wedding? The couple's history or socioeconomic situation?

APPLICATION ACTIVITY

Identify an everyday genre that you could bring into your L2 writing class as a way to explore genres. As in the wedding invitation example, try to find a genre that many of your students would be familiar with, but that they might have different experiences with (for example, using it in different languages or in different social/cultural contexts). Brainstorm a list of questions about the genre's rhetorical situation that you could give to your students for discussion.

Communities of Users

Communities of users play an especially important role in shaping genres. These communities are often called **discourse communities** to emphasize that the users share some preferences for using language. It is also good to remind students that communities are heterogeneous and include tensions and different viewpoints. This variation within communities is part of the reason we also see variations within genres.

We all participate in multiple discourse communities, in our personal lives, our work lives, and our educational lives. In order to communicate with members and to achieve community goals, discourse communities develop and adapt genres. For example, the writing program that I work in includes a large number of teachers, administrators, and staff. To communicate important information (such as changes to program policies, reminders of required tasks, or announcements of upcoming events), we have developed a specific genre: the program announcement email.

It is not a formally developed genre, and different users may call it by different names. Nevertheless, it is recognizable by its email subject line (which typically starts with ANNOUNCEMENT: in all caps) and by certain features of the email message (e.g., salutation to readers, statement of what is being announced, use of bullets or short paragraphs to make it quickly readable, occasional use of boldface for key details). These features are not coincidental—they reflect the program's value in communicating information to everyone in written form, while managing the need to keep email messages short and easy to read.

Understanding a community can lead to valuable insight into how to use their genres. Likewise, understanding a community's genres can help one participate in the community. For students, communities may be as specific as a student organization or as broad as "the academic community." As students advance through their education or workplaces, they will begin to interact with increasingly specific disciplinary or professional communities, and they will encounter new genres used by those communities.

Identities

By now it may be apparent that when we write in a genre, we take on practices, frames of mind, hopes, and orientations of the kind of people who write in that genre (Bazerman, 2002). Through genres, we adopt—and even develop—identities. For example, when I write an announcement to my writing program listserv, I am taking on the identity of a member of my writing program community. If my announcement is a policy reminder, my identity as a program administrator is highlighted. If my announcement is related to teaching L2 writing, my identity as an L2 writing specialist is foregrounded.

Learning to write new genres can be especially challenging when it requires taking on a new identity. For example, university writing may ask students to write as disciplinary members when they are still very new to a discipline. Graduate-level writing often requires students to write in the genres of disciplinary experts: research articles, proposals, conference proposals, or posters, for example.

In a genre-based writing class, we can introduce genres that will add to students' repertoires of roles and identities as writers. Instead of asking them to write only as students—in genres like argument essays—we can offer them practice with genres that assign them new roles and perhaps even highlight other aspects of their identities (see also Jacobson, 2019; Johns, 1997). For example, consider the difference between students writing an argumentative essay versus an opinion piece for a student newspaper. The two texts could address the same topic and goals, but one is written solely for a teacher and grade while in the latter, students can temporarily adopt an identity of an informed community member or as someone with relevant personal experience, drawing on their own resources and experiences as legitimate resources for writing.

Of course, students need practice in writing as students as well. Even when writing in more typical school-based genres, students can consider how other aspects of their identities might be used in effective ways. For example, international or immigrant students might consider how they can use their identities as transnational or multilingual individuals in effective and valued ways within different genres.

Classroom Exploration

There are numerous ways in which students might explore the social and rhetorical aspects of genre within a writing classroom. Tasks like those listed help students identify social and rhetorical features of a genre while connecting those to a genre's possible forms.

- *Comparing genre samples across communities or contexts*: One relatively simple way to highlight how genres are shaped by community users is to ask students to compare samples of a genre across two or three communities. Choose a genre that is used by multiple groups or in multiple contexts. For example, you might choose look at sample book reviews written in science journals versus humanities journals. To compare genres across contexts, students could compare online reviews of restaurants versus medical services. Students can compare similarities and differences across the sub-genres and then try to identify why these differences might exist, taking into account differences in communities or contexts.
- *Annotate a sample genre*: This activity works well after students have already learned more about a rhetorical situation or community. Ask them to annotate a sample genre (using in-text comments), noting features of the text that seem to be influenced by the situation or community. For example, they may make note of specialized vocabulary, insider content knowledge, a preference for short sentences, and so on. Alternatively, students can annotate a text to note aspects of the author's identity that are foregrounded through different features. A final variation is for students to annotate a genre text they have composed, noting some purposeful choices they made in their writing and connecting those choices to the community, context, or author identity.

7. Playing with Genres

So far, we have focused on ways for students to learn more about the conventions of genres and how those conventions are shaped by their contexts, communities, and social practices. This chapter focuses on the powerful role that *play* can take in learning conventions and in learning how to exploit those conventions.

Why Play?

There are several reasons to take seriously the potential role of play in raising students' metacognitive genre awareness and in building their genre-specific knowledge. **Genre play** can be considered a kind of **language play**, which has been defined by Tarone (2002) as "the expression of the speaker's creativity in deliberately, consciously choosing to violate normal expectancies of language use by playing off different varieties against one another, for the sheer purpose of enjoyment and entertainment" (p. 293). Corpus-based studies of language use have found language play to be pervasive in oral communication (e.g., Carter, 2004).

Research into language play identifies several potential ways in which such play might also support second language acquisition. Language play exemplifies the unpredictability of language use and helps learners see language as dynamic and open to change (Tarone, 2002). Its fun nature may also help make features of the L2 more noticeable and memorable (Tarone, 2000, 2002). Engaging in language play gives students freedom to experiment with unusual forms (Cekaite & Aronsson, 2005). When they engage in role play (a kind of language play), students can adopt new social roles, practicing variations in language and building sociolinguistic competence (Tarone, 2000, 2002); there is even some evidence that students' grammatical accuracy may improve when adopting certain roles and voices (LaScotte & Tarone, 2019). Language play also provides opportunities for authentic language use, preparing students for the kind of interactions that might take place outside of classrooms (Cekaite & Aronsson, 2005).

Though most studies of language play have focused on oral language, the general practices and principles are easily adapted to written language use. Genre play, as Hyon (2018) notes, "involves a speaker's or writer's purposeful movement away from prototypical forms or functions of the genre s/he is using" (p. 163). Playing with genres can help highlight for students the variation inherent to genre. When engaging with such variation in a playful manner, learning may be more pleasurable and perhaps even more memorable (Tarone, 2000). Students can practice using genres from new roles and identities, experimenting with ways in which language can represent writers and readers.

Exploring variations and even playful innovations to genres also implicitly highlights genre conventions. Students learn what is common, optional, rare, or risky. They explore where and when certain variations might occur, and by whom. In doing so, they are enriching their understanding of specific genres, while also expanding their broader awareness of genres. Genre play would therefore seem to support a broader goal of helping students develop rhetorical flexibility so that they can adapt "their socio-cognitive genre knowledge to ever-evolving contexts" (Johns, 2008, p. 239).

Bending Genres

Highlighting variation in genre samples is essential in a genre-based approach. Without explicit attention to variation, genre may become (to students or teachers) a fancy word for formula or template. A focus on variation also helps writers see that authors make *choices* as they write, selecting from among a set of preferred options.

Sometimes genre texts vary more significantly and may be considered outliers or innovations. Genre innovation can occur in numerous areas of a genre, as these examples show (Tardy, 2016, p. 131):

- Linguistic and textual form: *Unusual word choices; non-canonical grammar forms; mixing of linguistic codes; unconventional move structures*
- Modality: *Integration of unconventional modalities; use of an uncommon modality for that genre*
- Rhetorical aims and strategies: *Unconventional use of stance or engagement markers; use of rhetorical appeals uncommon to the genre*
- Content: *Incorporation of unusual or unexpected ideas*
- Practice: *Unique approaches to research methodology, design, or composing processes*

When exploring a genre, students can also examine its variations and possible innovations. Some classroom tasks for facilitating such exploration might include:

- *Consider possibilities for variation*: Ask students to consider a range of genres, such as autobiographies, annotated bibliographies, book reviews, business case study reports, in-class exams exams, lab reports, and reading summaries. They should place these genres on a continuum from "low flexibility" to "high flexibility," considering how open to variation each genre is. After comparing their responses, students can discuss what leads different genres to be more flexible than others, what kinds of variation are common (or rare), and what might influence how much an individual writer can vary a genre (Tardy, 2016, p. 148).
- *Identifying outliers*: Students can try to find outlier examples of a genre. These might be playful texts that include an unusual feature, or they could even be examples that are so far from the genre "prototype" that it is unclear whether they belong in the genre category. Once students have found outliers or innovations, they can try to understand the rhetorical context of the sample—What was unique about this text? Why did the author make these choices?—and discuss the extent to which they think the innovation would be effective, and why or why not.
- *Bend a feature in a genre for a given purpose*: Identify a few common features of a genre that you have explored as a class, and consider when, why, and how writers might bend those conventions. For example, if when exploring a genre that rarely uses first-person pronouns, students might discuss what would happen in that genre if a writer did use *I/me/my*. They could rewrite portions of the text by bending the convention, and then consider the effects of this change. This activity should lead to discussion about who can bend convention and why they might purposefully choose to do so.

Parody

Parody relies on genre, as it is primarily an ironic use of a genre, exploiting (often through exaggeration) certain genre features. Swales (1990) has long advocated for the value of parody in teaching academic writing, because parody relies on knowledge of convention and community. Parody is also playful, taking students beyond the seriousness of learning academic writing and highlighting instead the ways that writers can exploit texts for their own purposes.

In my experience, writing a parody can be fairly challenging for students, but it can also be an excellent activity for learning about genre conventions and about the social and rhetorical aspects of a genre. Parodies might be written for genres as short as academic article titles or for parts of longer genres, such as methodology descriptions. A miniature version of parody for research methodology sections can be found in the Twitter hashtag #overlyhonestmethods. Even very short parodies like this can highlight the values of a genre and the reasons that certain forms are preferred.

Parody texts can be composed collaboratively as a class, in small groups, or individually. Students can even rate each others' parodies for effectiveness. That said, the main purpose for incorporating parody is not to compose perfect parodies, but rather to better understand the formal conventions and social worlds of genres.

Role Play

Role play is a common activity in language classrooms, though it tends to be rare in writing instruction. Yet, as a form of language play, role play has a great deal of potential for learning about genres. Through simulated scenarios, students have the opportunity to write from different roles, take on new identities, and consider audiences beyond the classroom. A detailed role play can give students practice in responding to specific rhetorical situations. The following examples illustrate how role play may be integrated into a writing classroom:

- *Re-write a text for a new rhetorical situation*: After exploring some
  samples of a genre, the teacher can give students a unique (and
  perhaps humorous) rhetorical situation. Perhaps, for example, you
  are teaching emails of request. After exploring numerous examples,
  you could give students a rather specific rhetorical situation: *You are a
  graduate student working on a project for a seminar. Professor Fancier is
  a renowned academic who has published in this area. You are unable to
  access an obscure but famous paper by Prof. Fancier on this topic, and your
  supervisor has (perhaps unwisely) suggested that you write her to request*

a copy of the paper. Write your email of request. After composing their texts, students can compare their approaches and discuss which text would likely receive a positive response and why.

- *Write or annotate a text from a specific identity position*: Students often write from the position of students or novices. To give them an opportunity to practice new forms—which they may feel are unavailable to novices—give them new identities. For example, graduate students may re-write parts of their literature review, imagining that they are a well-respected scholar in this area. Alternatively, they could annotate their existing text and note how they might write differently if they were a more established scholar.

Remixing and Redesigning

Remixing and redesigning have become fairly common assignments in many writing classrooms. These tasks of taking content developed for one genre and re-shaping it for a new genre usefully engage students with questions about how contexts, communities, and genres influence writing choices. As such, students can learn more about the individual genres they are working with, while also building a broader genre awareness and, ultimately, their rhetorical flexibility as writers. Remixing and redesigning can be considered a kind of genre play, especially when they encourage students to be playful in their redesign

Remixing can be as simple as changing the mode of a genre. For example, students can remix a written summary into a short video note for a class digital discussion forum. They can consider what might need to change—in their content, organization, sentence structure, word choice, etc.—through this relatively small shift in delivery.

Remixing can also be more complex. Students might create an academic poster or video abstract from a lengthier source-based argument, for example. In these cases, writers need to learn about both genres and compare their contexts, communities, purposes, and forms.

After remixing a genre, it is useful for students to explicitly reflect on the changes that they made and why. Such reflections do not need to be lengthy or formal; they can take the form of visuals, lists, Venn diagrams, or even pod-casts or screencasts. The key is that students articulate the differences in the genres (or modes) and how those differences affected the choices they made.

My colleagues Jeroen Gevers, Shelley Staples, and I have tried to incorporate students' multilingual backgrounds into a remixing assignment as well. After completing a literature review assignment in our first-year university writing course, we asked our students to adapt the content from their literature review into one of three public genres: a public blog (for prospective or current international students), an infographic, or a public letter in an educational context. We first had students select a genre, collect samples in English, and work through a series of analysis tasks, so that they became familiar with the genre they had chosen. Next, we asked them to find three to five examples of the same genre in their first languages and to work through the same analysis tasks for those texts. After analyzing the genre samples in both languages, they created a Venn diagram noting the features that were unique to each language and those that were shared across languages (an idea adapted from Johns, 2015). Finally, students had to create a sample of the genre in English and their L1 and write a short explanation of the choices that they made in each language.

Remixing across modes, languages, and communities allows students to engage directly with the flexibility of language and writing, while requiring them to think through genre features and adaptations.

APPLICATION ACTIVITY

Consider a genre that you have taught or would like to teach to students. What are two activities you could use in class that will allow for playful adaptation or exploitation of that genre? How might they contribute to students' genre knowledge and genre awareness? If possible, design two classroom tasks and share them with a colleague.

8. Final Tips for Teachers

Teachers often tell me that they are intimidated by genre and are unsure if they understand what it is or how to bring it into their classrooms. As shown in the previous chapter, genre can simply be a lens for understanding writing. It can help students—and teachers—explore familiar and unfamiliar kinds of writing, learning more about texts, their contexts, and how the two influence each other.

Genre-based writing instruction aims to build students' genre knowledge and genre awareness through guided exploration of sample genres. It strives to raise students' awareness of the flexibility and goal-oriented nature of written communication, while helping them build their own repertoire of linguistic and rhetorical strategies for such communication. This book has provided some tools for implementing genre-based writing instruction and has offered several practical ideas for classroom tasks. The book concludes with seven final tips for teachers who wish to bring a genre-based approach to their writing classrooms.

Tip 1: Scaffold.

As noted, scaffolding is a central principle of genre-based teaching. Learning genres involves more than learning a form, as we have seen. Rather than having students explore forms, content, social practices, and rhetorical features all at once, it is useful to scaffold these explorations. Scaffolding might include "modelling and discussion of texts, explicit instruction, and teacher input" (Hyland, 2007, p. 158).

Scaffolding also involves returning to similar types of exploratory tasks with new genres throughout a course. For example, students might engage in rhetorical moves analysis each time they explore a new genre. New questions or approaches to moves analysis can be added as they become more comfortable with this task in different genres.

Teachers can think broadly about where they want students to be at the end of a course, including what they want students to know about specific genres (genre knowledge) and about genres and genre analysis more generally (genre awareness). Then comes the challenging job of sequencing and scaffolding tasks throughout a course to gradually build such knowledge and awareness. Genre learning does not happen in one assignment or even in a few tasks—rather, it is built over time through repeated practice

Tip 2: Don't overcomplicate.

Although genre is a relatively complex concept in some ways, it is also fairly straightforward in other ways: Genres help us do things, and they vary (in their form and practices, among other areas) in accordance with what they are doing, for whom, and when. This basic idea is not challenging for students to grasp, and it should be at the heart of genre teaching.

Genre theory tends to emphasize the complexity of genre, and that is useful in many cases. However, in my experience, it is not necessary to engage students with this level of complexity, especially when they are first grappling with the concept. In fact, in some L2 writing classes I have taught, I have avoided the term *genre* entirely. My main goal, instead, is to help students see the social and situated nature of writing and to practice some tools for exploring how social features influence textual choices.

It can be valuable to give students some metalanguage for such explorations, but in general I have not found it useful to ask students to read through complicated explanations of what genres are, or how different genre scholars have defined them. Instead, I try to focus on designing well-sequenced, engaging, and even fun, tasks that help students uncover these complexities themselves.

Tip 3: Don't oversimplify.

Perhaps somewhat in contrast to Tip 2, I think it is also important not to over-simplify. Here, the primary danger is that students may start to see genres as just another template or structure for writing, similar to a five-paragraph essay or other formula that they may have learned. It is important to engage students with variations and even radical innovations because it is these departures from prototypes that allow individuals to use genres for their own purposes.

Tip 4: Focus on exploration.

A genre-based approach to writing instruction is not primarily about teaching students different genres. Instead, it is about teaching students how to explore genres, as a means of raising their rhetorical consciousness as writers. Student-driven exploration of genres is therefore at the heart of genre-based pedagogy. Classroom teaching that consistently engages students in exploratory tasks teaches them how to look at texts and how to bring those insights to their writing.

Tip 5: Create a genre-rich and text-rich classroom.

Because of the emphasis on exploration, genre-based classrooms often include multiple genres and numerous text samples of each. Even courses focused primarily on a single genre (such as a dissertation or thesis) can benefit from exploration of related genres. By seeing genres as parts of networks, or by comparing how different genres function for users, students gain a broader understanding of writing and build genre awareness. By exploring both everyday genres and school or professional genres, students can also begin to see that all writing involves choices that take into account social context and users.

Because highlighting genre variation is essential, it is not enough to include just two or three examples of a genre that students will explore. Indeed, finding sample texts can often be the most time-consuming part of genre pedagogy. Over time, however, teachers can accrue increasingly rich genre collections, and student-selected samples can contribute to these collections as well.

Perhaps implicit in this discussion is the need to move our L2 writing classrooms beyond "essay writing" as the primary or even sole text type that we teach and allows students to produce. While the "school essay" is a form that they will find necessary to use in some tasks, such as timed exams (Johns, 2008), we also need to engage students with the rich and varied nature of writing and give them opportunities to explore the range of genres that people use to achieve various aims.

Tip 6: Make learning explicit.

Research into metacognition suggests that there are learning benefits to helping students consolidate their knowledge (e.g., Negretti & McGrath, 2018), and this often takes the form of articulating what they know. Explicit articulations of learning do not need to take the form of lengthy reflections.

Simple self-annotations of students' writing or sample writing (e.g., Cheng, 2018) can serve the same purpose, giving learners a chance to indicate what they know in a low-stakes form. Articulations of learning and knowledge can also take the form of visualizations (Negretti & McGrath, 2018), or concept maps (Wette, 2017), which allow students to focus on their content knowledge without worrying about language use. What matters is that they have some opportunity to reflect on their learning and to make that learning explicit in some way, thereby facilitating the likelihood that they will be able to adapt that knowledge to new writing tasks.

Tip 7: Teach for genre-specific knowledge and genre awareness.

Primary goals for writing courses will differ according to the educational context. In a workplace class, the aim may be for students to write an internal monthly report effectively; in an early undergraduate class, the aim may be more broadly to prepare students for university writing, in all its variations. Therefore, the focus on genre-specific knowledge may be stronger in the first scenario, while an emphasis on metacognitive genre awareness may be more prominent in the second scenario. That said, research suggests that our genre awareness is enriched by experience with specific genres, and a broad understanding of genres can enrich our genre-specific knowledge (Cheng, 2018; Yasuda, 2011). As teachers of writing, we can keep an eye on both of these related concepts through the kinds of tasks and practices described here.

REFERENCES

Bawarshi, A. S. (2003). *Genre and the invention of the writer: Reconsidering the place of invention in composition.* Logan: Utah State University Press.

Bazerman, C. (2002). Genre and identity: Citizenship in the age of the internet and the age of global capitalism. In R. Coe, L. Lingard, & T. Teslenko (Eds.), *The rhetoric and ideology of genre* (pp. 13–37). Creskill, NJ: Hampton Press.

Caplan, N. A., & Farling, M. (2016). A dozen heads are better than one: Collaborative writing in genre-based pedagogy. *TESOL Journal, 8,* 564–581.

Carter, R. (2004). *Language and creativity: The art of common talk.* London: Routledge.

Cekaite, A., & Aronsson, K. (2005). Language play, a collaborative resource in children's L2 learning. *Applied Linguistics, 26*(2), 169–191.

Cheng, A. (2018). *Genre and graduate-level research writing.* Ann Arbor: University of Michigan Press.

Devitt, A. (2009). Teaching critical genre awareness. In C. Bazerman, A. Bonini, & D Figueiredo (Eds.), *Genre in a changing world: Perspectives on writing* (pp. 337–351). Fort Collins, CO: The WAC Clearinghouse and Parlor Press.

Feak, C. B., & Swales, J. M. (2009). *Telling a research story: Writing a literature review.* Ann Arbor: University of Michigan Press.

Freadman, A. (1987). Anyone for tennis? In I. Reid (Ed.), *The place of genre in learning: Current debates* (pp. 91–124). Geelong, Australia: Deakin University Centre for Studies in Literary Education.

Gentil, G. (2011). A biliteracy agenda for genre research. *Journal of Second Language Writing, 20,* 6–23.

Hyland, K. (2004). *Genre and second language writing.* Ann Arbor: University of Michigan Press.

Hyland, K. (2007). Genre pedagogy: Language, literacy, and L2 writing instruction. *Journal of Second Language Writing, 16,* 148–164.

Hyon, S. (2018). *Introducing genre and English for specific purposes.* New York: Routledge.

Jacobson, B. (2019). Negotiating transitions: A genre-based study of writing opportunities across high school and college (Unpublished doctoral dissertation). University of Arizona, Tucson.

James, M. A. (2008). The influence of perceptions of task similarity/difference on learning transfer in second language writing. *Written Communication*, *25*, 76–103.

Johns, A. M. (1997). *Text, role, and context: Developing academic literacies.* New York: Cambridge University Press.

Johns, A. M. (2008). Genre awareness for the novice academic student: An ongoing quest. *Language Teaching*, *41*(2), 237–252.

Johns, A. M. (2015). Moving on from *Genre Analysis*: An update and tasks for the transitional student. *Journal of English for Academic Purposes*, *19*, 113–124.

Korsós, G., Horváth, K., Lukács, A., Vezér, T., Glávits, R., Fodor, K., & Fekete, S. G. (2018). Effects of accelerated human music on learning and memory performance of rats. *Applied Animal Behaviour Science*, *202*, 94–99.

LaScotte, D., & Tarone, E. (2019). Heteroglossia and constructed dialogue in SLA. *The Modern Language Journal*, *103*, 95–112.

Martin, J. R. (1984). Language, register, and genre. In F. Christie (Ed.), *Language studies: Children's writing, reader.* Geelong, Australia: Deakin University Press.

Miller, C. R. (1984). Genre as social action. *Quarterly Journal of Speech*, *70*, 151–167.

Myers, G. (1990). *Writing biology: Texts in the construction of scientific knowledge.* Madison: University of Wisconsin Press.

Negretti, R., & McGrath, L. (2018). Scaffolding genre knowledge and metacognition: Insights from an L2 doctoral research writing course. *Journal of Second Language Writing*, *40*, 12–31.

Rose, D., & Martin, J. R. (2012). *Learning to write, reading to learn: Genre, knowledge and pedagogy in the Sydney School.* Bristol, CT: Equinox.

Russell, D. R., & Fisher, D. (2009). Online, multimedia case studies for professional education: Revisioning concepts of genre recognition. In J. Giltrow & D. Stein (Eds.), *Genres in the internet: Issues in the theory of genre* (pp. 163–192). Philadelphia, PA: John Benjamins.

Swain, M. (1993). The output hypothesis: Just speaking and writing aren't enough. *The Canadian Modern Language Review*, *50*, 158–164.

Swales, J. M. (1990). *Genre analysis: English in academic and research settings.* Cambridge, England: Cambridge University Press.

Swales, J. M. (2009). When there is no perfect text: Approaches to the EAP practitioner's dilemma. *Journal of English for Academic Purposes, 8*, 5–13.

Swales, J. M., & Feak, C. B. (2009). *Abstracts and the writing of abstracts: Revised/ expanded English in today's research world.* Ann Arbor: University of Michigan Press.

Swales, J. M., & Feak, C. B. (2011). *Navigating academic: Writing supporting genres.* Ann Arbor: University of Michigan Press.

Swales, J. M., & Feak, C. B. (2012). *Academic writing tasks for graduate students* (3rd ed.). Ann Arbor: University of Michigan Press.

Tardy, C. M. (2009). *Building genre knowledge.* West Lafayette, IN: Parlor Press.

Tardy, C. M. (2016). *Beyond convention: Genre innovation in academic writing.* Ann Arbor: University of Michigan Press.

Tarone, E. (2000). Getting serious about language play: Language play, interlanguage variation and second language acquisition. In B. Swierzbein, F. Morris, M. Anderson, C. Klee, & E. Tarone (Eds.), *Social and cognitive factors in second language acquisition* (pp. 31–54). Somerville, CA: Cascadilla Press.

Tarone, E. (2002). Frequency effects, noticing, and creativity: Factors in a variationist interlanguage framework. *SSLA, 24*, 287–296.

Wette, R. (2017). Using mind maps to reveal and develop genre knowledge in a graduate writing course. *Journal of Second Language Writing, 38*, 58–71.

Yasuda, S. (2011). Genre-based tasks in foreign language writing: Developing writers' genre awareness, linguistic knowledge, and writing competence. *Journal of Second Language Writing, 20*, 111–133.